Baking a Cake

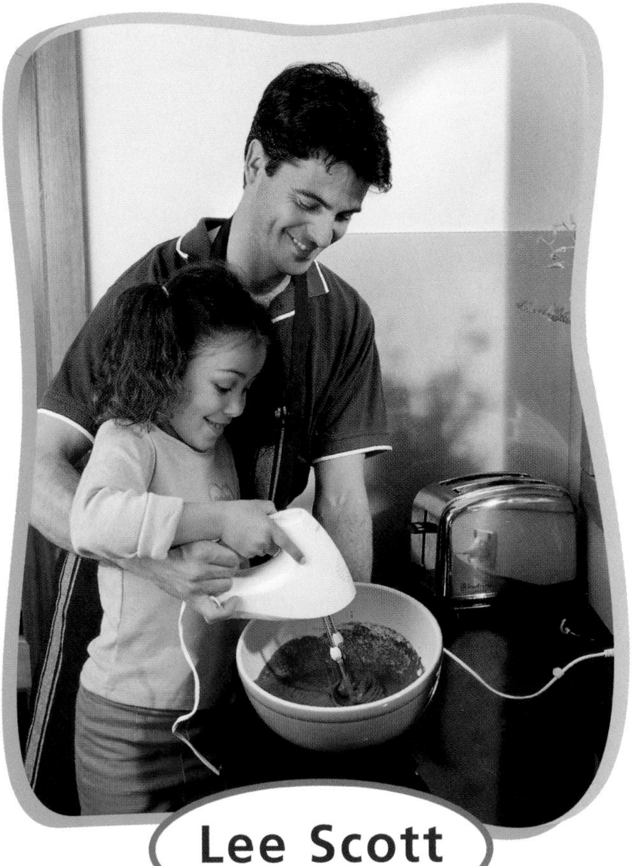

Lee Scott

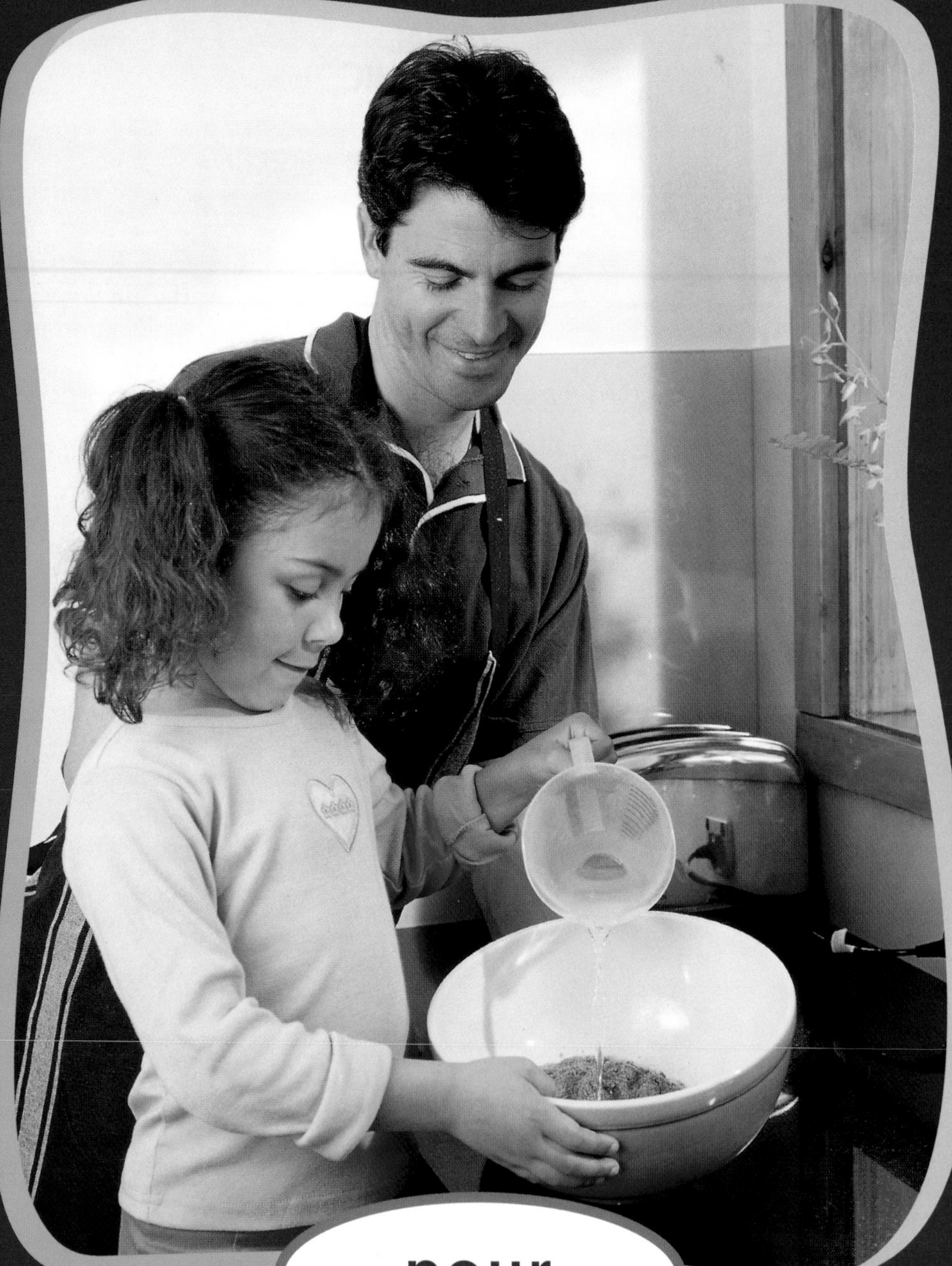

pour

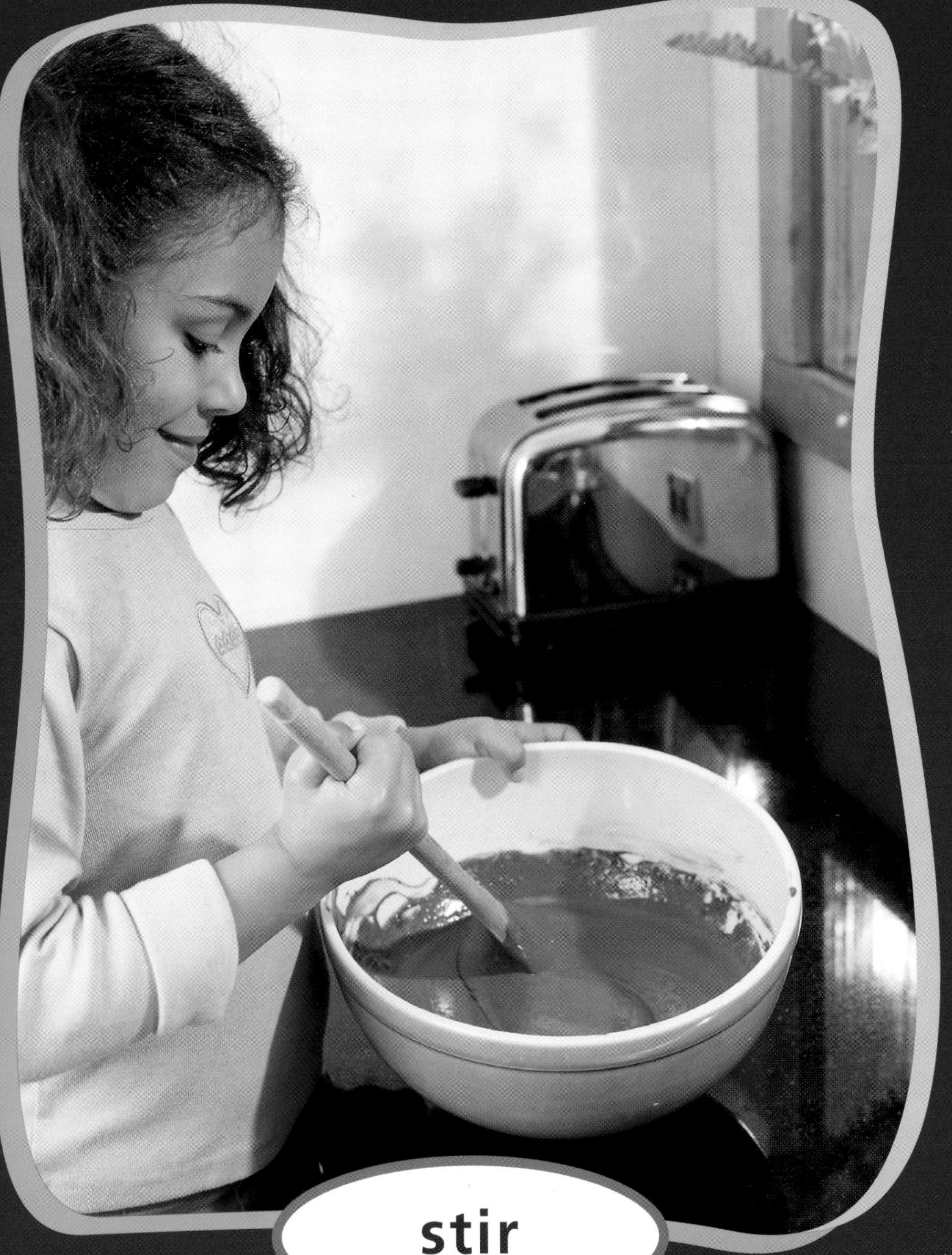

stir

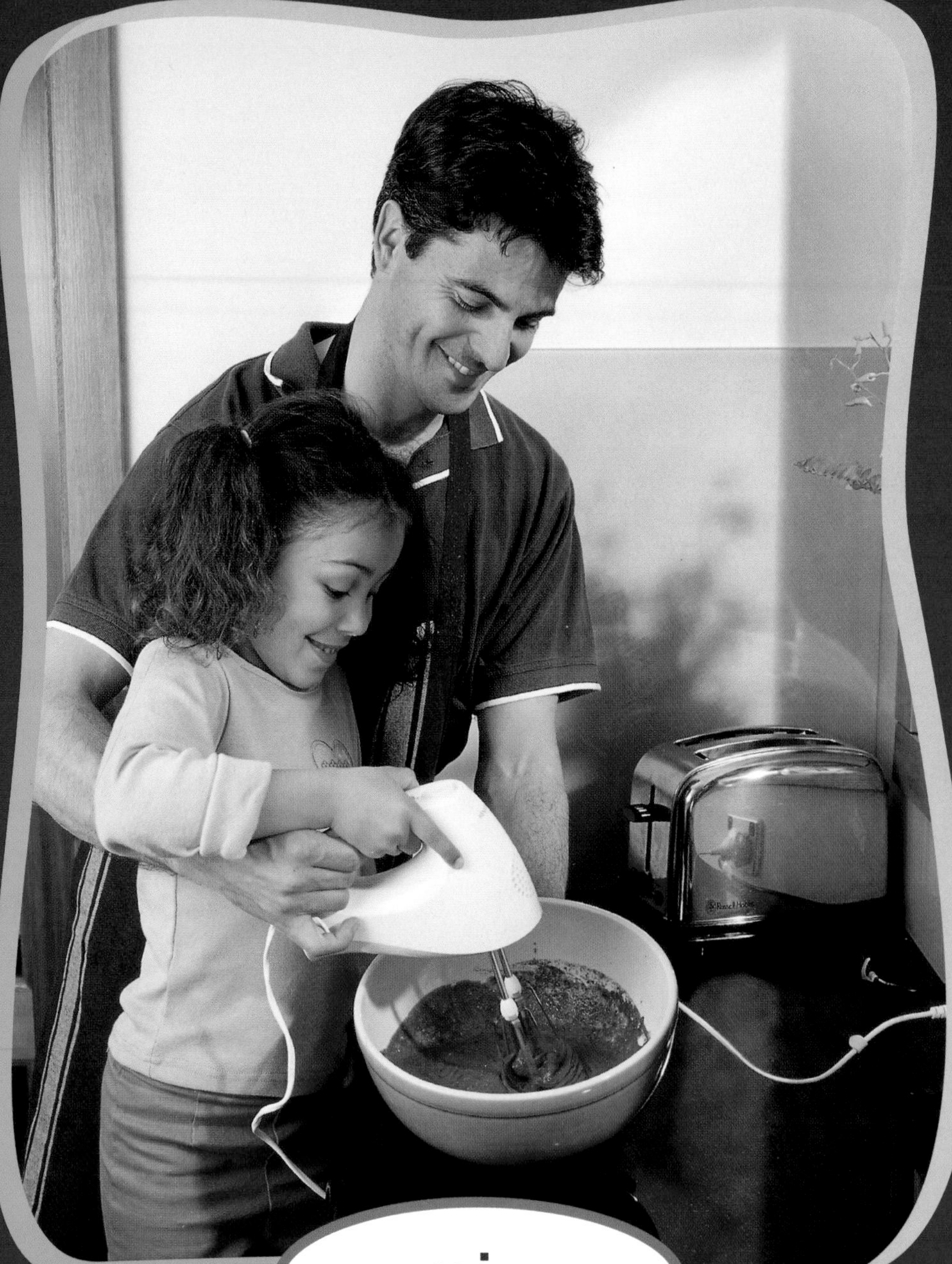

mix

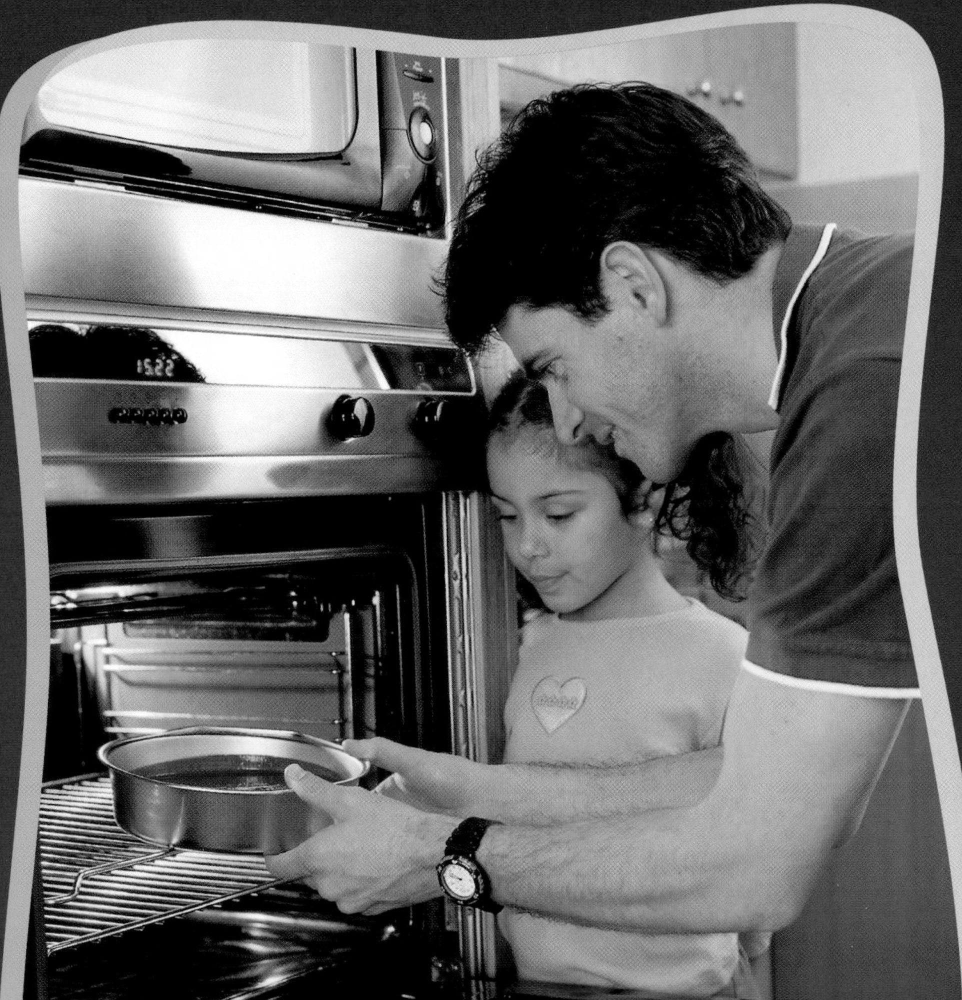

bake

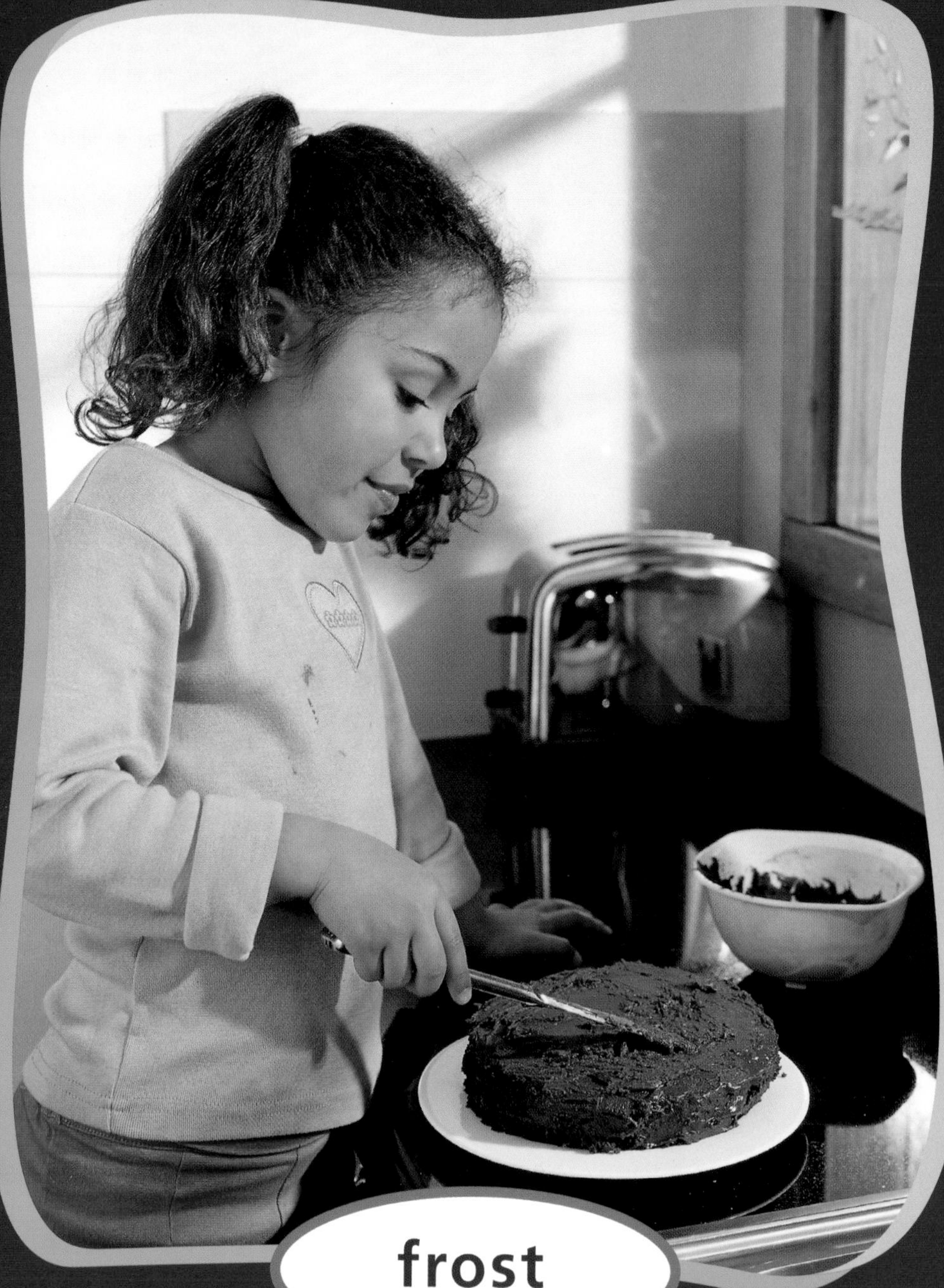

frost

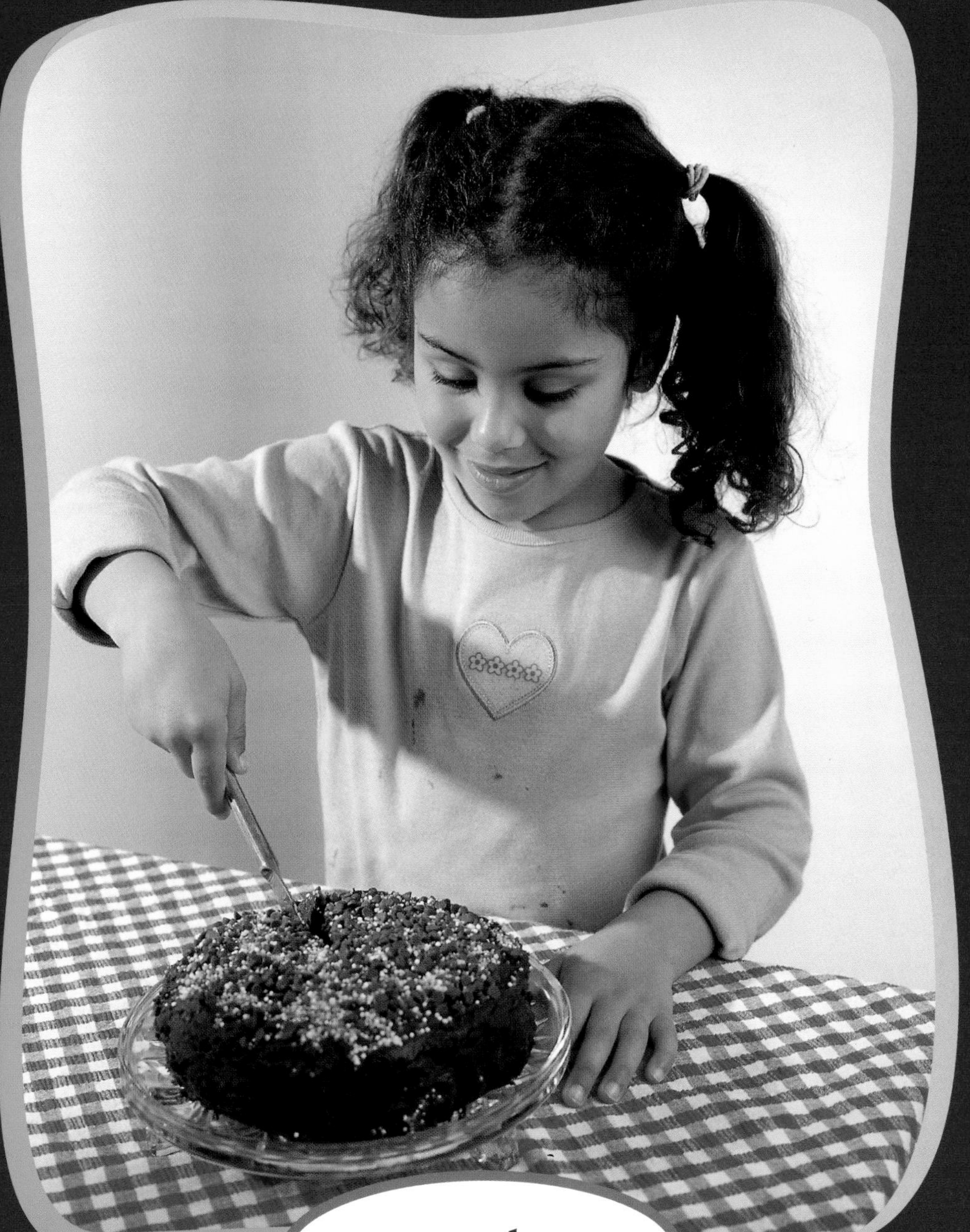

cut

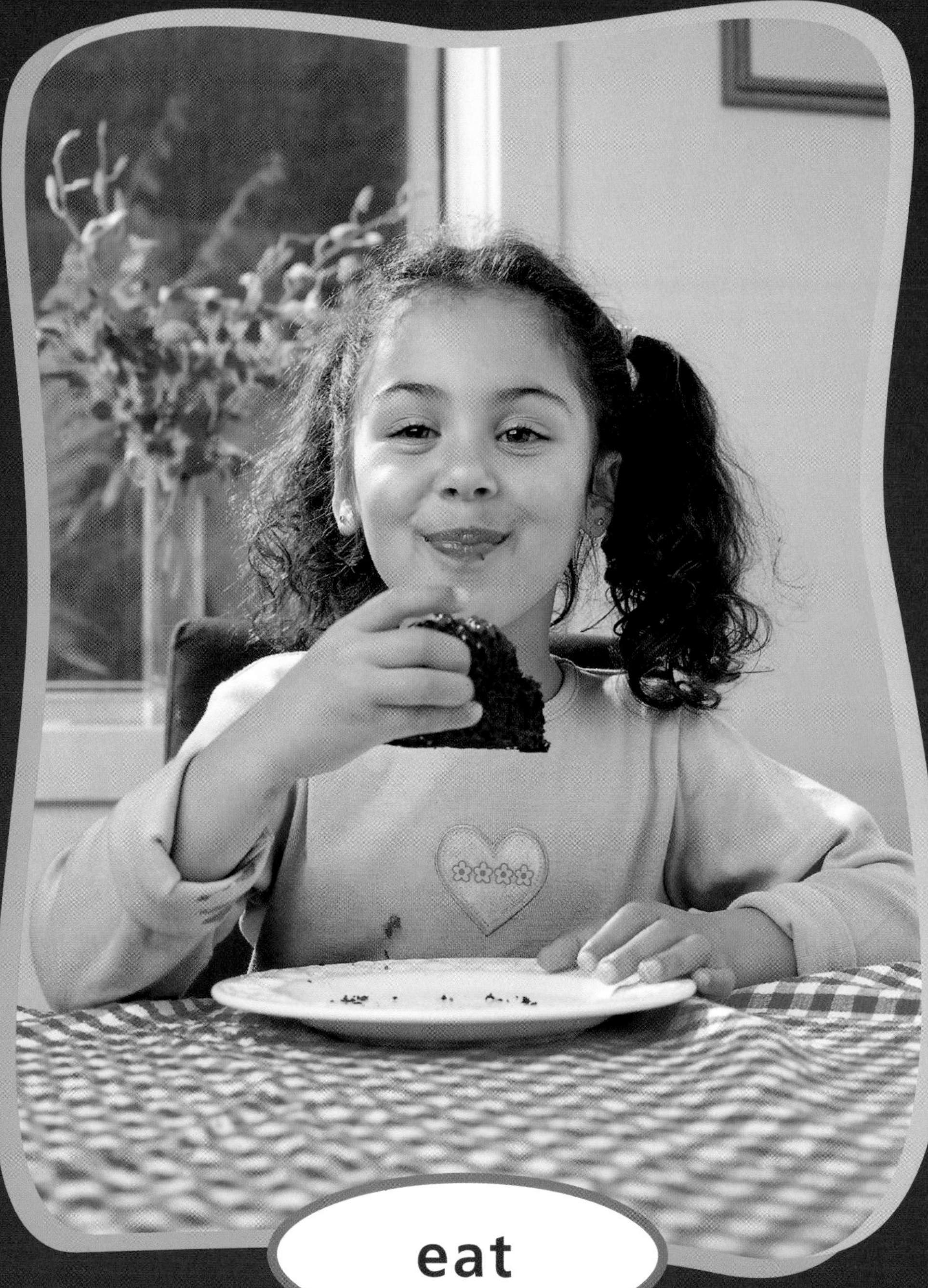

eat